MathStart™
ESTIMATING

BETCHA!

by Stuart J. Murphy • illustrated by S. D. Schindler

SCHOLASTIC INC.
New York Toronto London Auckland Sydney

LEVEL
3

**To Katherine Brown Tegen—
who was willing to betcha
that MathStart would work.**

—S.J.M.

ISBN 0-590-03379-4

Text copyright © 1997 by Stuart J. Murphy. Illustrations copyright © 1997 by S. D. Schindler. All rights reserved. Published by Scholastic Inc., 555 Broadway, New York, NY 10012, by arrangement with HarperCollins Children's Books, a division of HarperCollins Publishers. MathStart™ is a trademark of HarperCollins Publishers Inc. SCHOLASTIC and associated logos are trademarks and/or registered trademarks of Scholastic Inc.

12 11 10 9 8 7 6 5 4   2 3/0

Printed in the U.S.A.   08

First Scholastic printing, March 1998

Hey! Look at this. Planet Toys is having a contest. Whoever guesses the correct number of jelly beans in the jar in their window wins two free tickets to the All-Star Game!

PLANET TOYS

Guess how many jelly beans are in me!

Oh, yeah?
Let's go down and check it out.

5

Betcha I can win.

Oh yeah? I'm really good at figuring things out.
I betcha that I'll win.

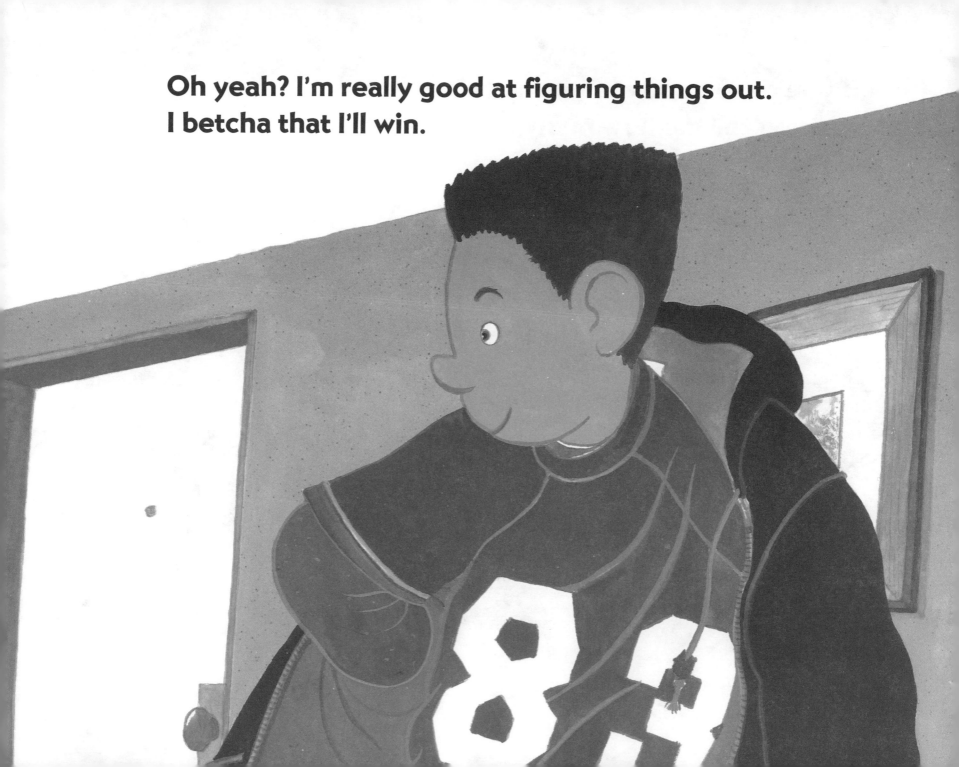

If you're so good at figuring things out, can you tell me how many other people are on this bus?

You betcha!

9

Okay. How many?

4 people → X

10 rows

= 40, plus a few standing up

Betcha about forty-three people.

12

I just counted, and I got forty-five.

I was pretty close!

Wow! Look at that traffic jam.
Betcha you can't tell me how many cars are
stuck on the block.

Betcha I can.

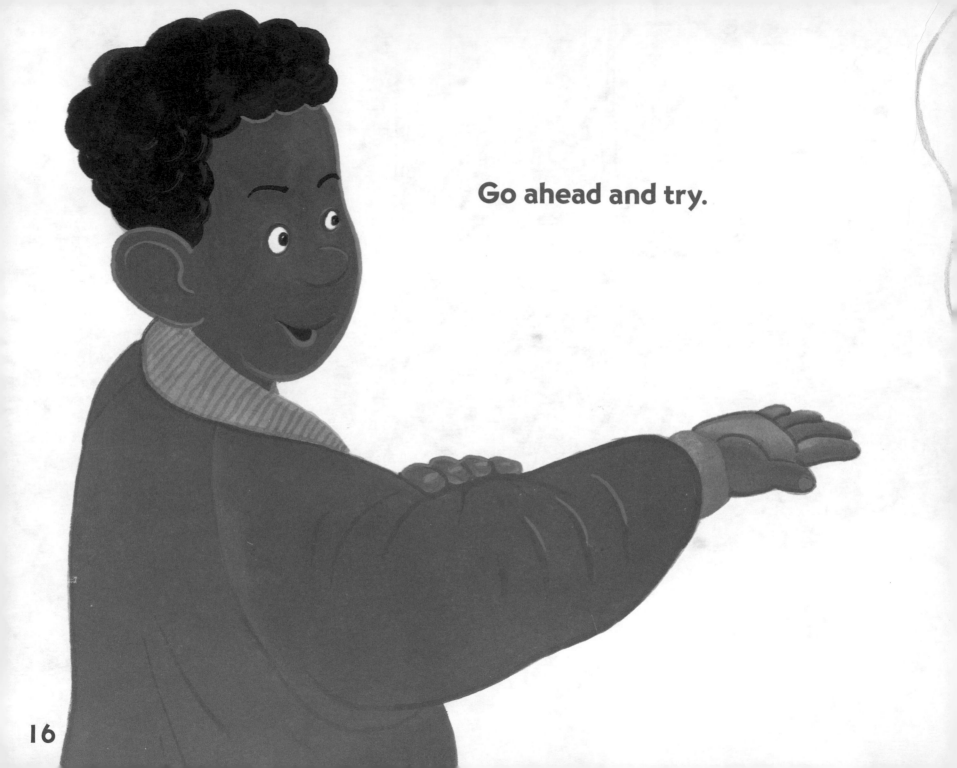

Go ahead and try.

16

6 cars

4 lanes

X

= 24

Betcha about twenty-five cars.

I counted twenty-three.

Here's the store. Look at all that cool stuff! About how much do you think it would cost to buy it all?

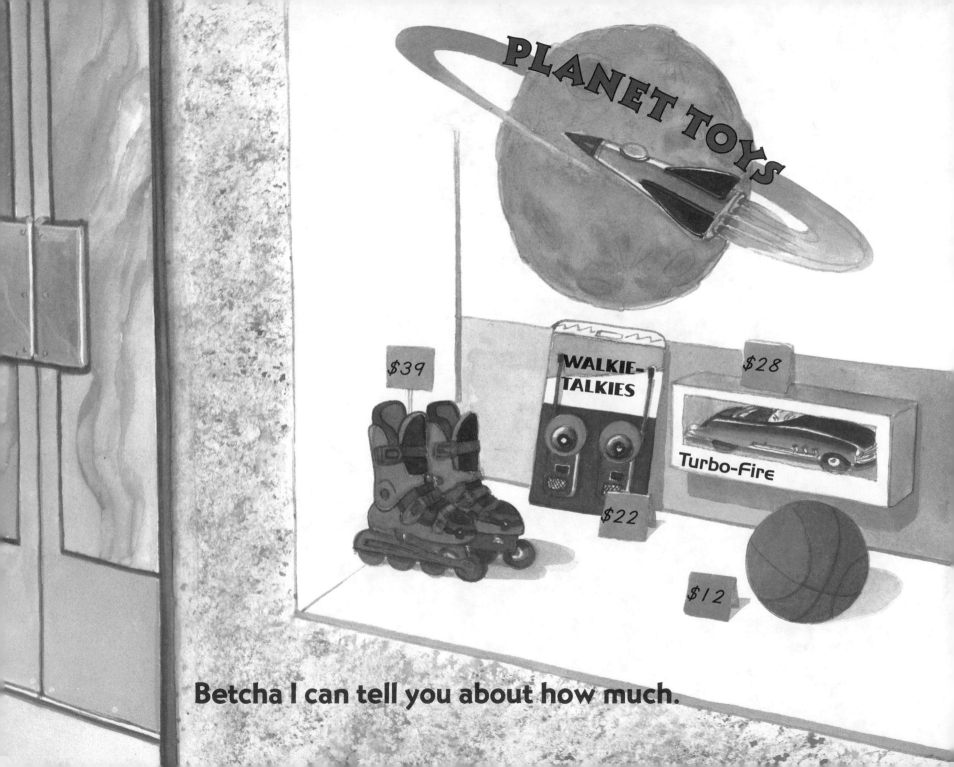

Betcha I can tell you about how much.

$39

WALKIE-TALKIES
$22

Turbo-Fire
$28

Almost $40 + just over $20 = about $60

$60 + almost $30 = about $90

$90 + just over $10
= about $100

$12

Betcha about $100.

See? I was close again,
and I didn't even need a pencil.

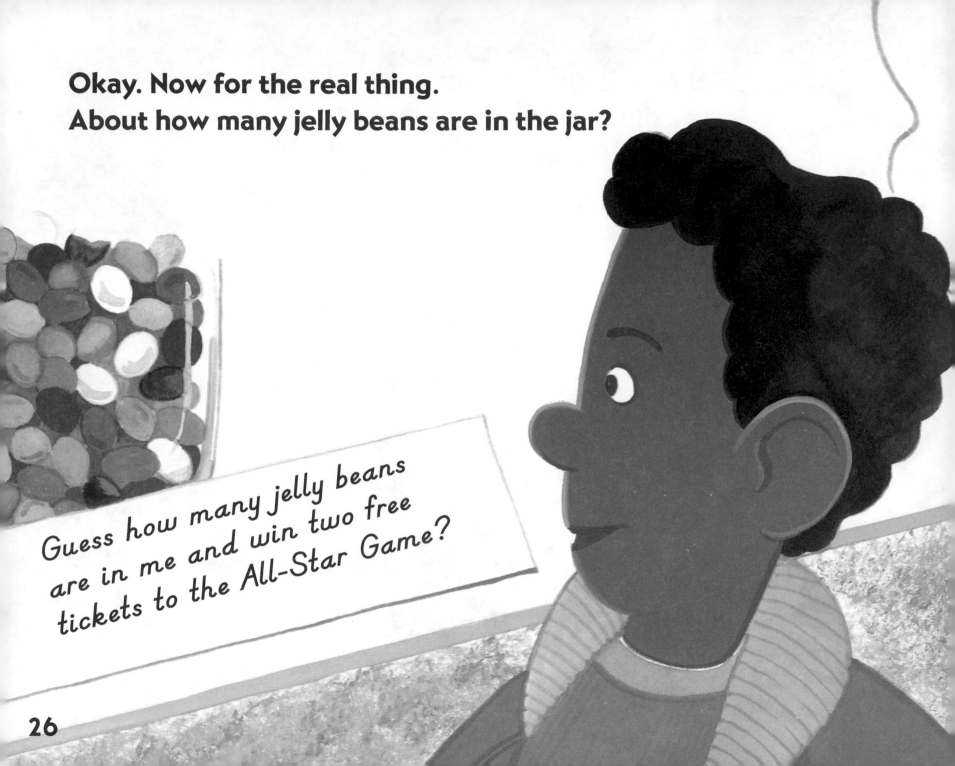

Okay. Now for the real thing.
About how many jelly beans are in the jar?

Guess how many jelly beans are in me and win two free tickets to the All-Star Game?

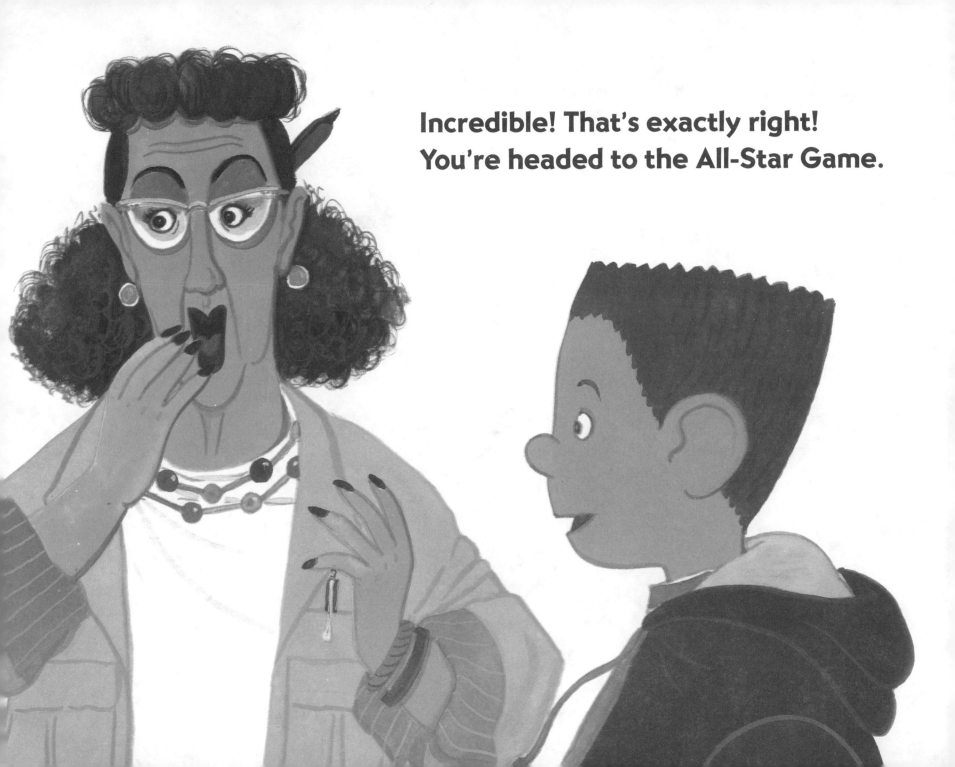

Incredible! That's exactly right!
You're headed to the All-Star Game.

Betcha I know who wants the other ticket!

If you would like to have more fun with the math concepts presented in *Betcha!*, here are a few suggestions:

- Read the story together and ask the child to describe what is going on in each picture. Ask questions throughout the story, such as "What would you do to estimate how many people are on a bus?" and "How would you estimate the number of cars in a traffic jam?"

- Help the child to understand what it means to estimate: Ask "How did you get your answer?" and "Is it about right?" Encourage the child to reconsider the estimate as more information is available. The process is more important than an exact answer.

- Discuss real-life situations that require estimations. Examples could include ordering enough pizza for the whole family or deciding how many errands can be done before ballet class or soccer practice.

- Try using estimation to check against calculator work. Estimate the total cost of four or five items in the refrigerator. Then add them up on a calculator. Was the estimate a reasonable answer? Was it about right? Try again with another group of items.

- Together, make up your own "Betcha!" game. Pick something that is difficult to count, such as people in a long line, cars in a parking lot, or cookies in a box. Help the child to consider different strategies for making these estimates. Then check to see how close these estimates are to the real numbers.

ollowing are some activities that will help you extend the concepts presented in *Betcha!* into a child's everyday life.

Eating Out: Estimate the number of people eating at a favorite restaurant. Do a quick count to see how close the estimate is. Try to estimate how many tables there are. How many chairs? About how much will the check total?

Taking a Walk: Estimate as you walk around your neighborhood. If you pass so many houses on one block, about how many houses will you pass after walking all the way to the park? If it takes a certain number of steps to walk between two lines on the sidewalk, about how many steps will it take to walk the entire length of the street? Around the block?

Buying Food: Estimate how much your family spends each month on one popular food item—cereal, for example. About how many boxes does your family eat each month? About how much does each box cost? About how much do you spend? Then keep track and see if your estimate is close.

he following books include some of the same concepts that are presented in *Betcha!*:

- COUNTING ON FRANK by Rod Clement

- COUNTING JENNIE by Helena Clare Pittman

- HOW MUCH IS A MILLION? by David M. Schwartz